W9-DBH-323

MAR

2011

CUTTING-EDGE SCIENCE

DRUG RESISTANCE

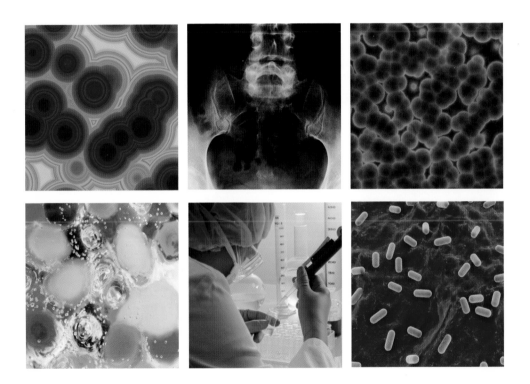

By Caroline Green

NEW FOREST PRESS

Publisher: Melissa Fairley
Editor: Miranda Smith
Designer: Helen Worgan
Production Controller: Ed Green
Production Manager: Suzy Kelly

ISBN: 978-1-84898-323-6
Library of Congress Control Number: 2010925196
Tracking number: nfp00001

North American edition copyright © *TickTock* Entertainment Ltd. 2010
First published in North America in 2010 by *New Forest Press*,
PO Box 784, Mankato, MN 56002
www.newforestpress.com

Printed in the USA
9 8 7 6 5 4 3 2 1

Picture credits (t=top; b=bottom; c=center; OFC= outside front cover; OBC=outside back cover):
Hazel Appleton, Center for Infections/Health Protection Agency/Science Photo Library: 41b. Thierry
Berrod, Mona Lisa Production/Science Photo Library: 44t. Borderlands/Alamy: 42–43. Andy Crump,
TDR, WHO/Science Photo Library: 57b. Design Pics Inc./Alamy: 50t. A. B. Dowsett/Science Photo
Library: 6–7t, 12t. Reza Estakhrian/Getty Images: 29t. David R. Frazier/Science Photo Library:
30–31. Steve Gschmeissner/Science Photo Library: 6b. Paul Gunning/Science Photo Library: 39t.
Imagebroker/Alamy: 37. iStock: 3B (and throughout), 8–9, 27b, 35t, 55b, 56. Dr. Kari
Lounatmaa/Science Photo Library: 28. Philippe Plailly/Eurelios/Science Photo Library: 61.
Philippe Psaila/Science Photo Library: 47. Phil Matt/AgstockUSA/Science Photo Library: 32t.
Science Photo Library: 53. Shutterstock: OFC, 1 (all and throughout), 3D/E/H (and throughout),
4–5, 10–11, 13, 22, 23b, 24–25, 26t, 34–35b, 40t, 45b, 49b, 58t, 59t. Science Source/Science
Photo Library: 14t, 15t, 18t, 33t. Scott Sinklier/AgstockUSA/Science Photo Library: 54. SSPL via
Getty Images: 20b, 21b. St. Mary's Hospital Medical School/Science Photo Library: 19b. Mark
Thomas/Science Photo Library: 51b. Geoff Tompkinson/Science Photo Library: 16–17, 38t.
Sotiris Zafeiris/Science Photo Library: 48

NOTE TO READERS
The website addresses are correct at the time of publishing. However, due to the ever-changing
nature of the Internet, websites and content may change. Some websites can contain links that are
unsuitable for children. The publisher is not responsible for changes in content or website addresses.
We advise that Internet searches are supervised by an adult.

CONTENTS

INTRODUCTION

A Return to the Dark Ages? 4

The Bugs Fight Back..6

Revenge of the Superbugs 8

CHAPTER 1 ....UNDER THE MICROSCOPE

The World of the Microbe..10

Sharing the World 12

Evolution Over Time..14

CHAPTER 2 ....THE ANTIBIOTIC REVOLUTION

Development of Antibiotics..16

The Discovery of Antibiotics..18

The Golden Age of Antibiotics 20

A Wave of Optimism..22

CHAPTER 3..NEW STRATEGIES

Microbes Fight Back..24

The Misuse of Antibiotics..26

Getting Sick in the Hospital..28

CHAPTER 4 ...........................ENVIRONMENTAL DANGERS

Resistance and the Environment..30

The Environmental Connection..32

Is the World "Antibacterial Crazy"? 34

CHAPTER 5 ....FIGHTING DISEASE

Old Enemies, New Invaders..36

MRSA—Superbug 38

Emerging Threats..40

HIV/AIDS..42

Malaria 44

CHAPTER 6 ....TAKING CONTROL

Finding a Solution 46

Playing a Vital Role 48

Fighting MRSA 50

CHAPTER 7....................................PREVENTION AND CURE

Looking to the Future..52

Resistance and HIV/AIDS..54

Preventing Malaria..56

The Rogues' Gallery of Microbes 58

Where Do We Go From Here?..60

Glossary 62

Index..64

A RETURN TO THE DARK AGES?

IMAGINE THIS. ONE A MONDAY MORNING, A MAN IS SCRATCHED ON THE FINGER BY HIS PET CAT. THE FINGER STARTS TO SWELL AND WEEP PUS ON WEDNESDAY. BY FRIDAY, THE MAN HAS A HIGH TEMPERATURE AND IS ADMITTED TO THE HOSPITAL. BY SUNDAY, HE IS DEAD.

FIGHTING TO LIVE

It sounds like something from a horror movie, but before **antibiotics** were developed, people caught deadly infections from simple everyday wounds. The availability of antibiotics ushered in a whole new era, when humans could at last control harmful bugs. Other medical breakthroughs followed over the next decades, with the development of **vaccines** against killer **diseases** and the discovery of powerful drugs against **malaria**, a major cause of death in the developing world.

In fact, there was such a wave of optimism that experts began to predict a time when infectious diseases would be completely wiped out. In 1978, scientists from 134 countries held the International Conference on Primary Health Care in Alma-Ata, Kazakhstan. The conference had an ambitious goal—"health for all"—and concluded that "an acceptable level of health for all the people of the world by the year 2000 can be attained."

Yet, in the 21st century, 17 million people are still dying from infectious diseases every day, according to the World Health Organization (**WHO**). Around 90 percent of these deaths are caused by only a few diseases. Six deadly infectious diseases— pneumonia, **tuberculosis (TB)**, diarrheal diseases, malaria, measles, and **HIV/AIDS**—account for one half of all premature deaths, mostly killing children and young adults. Drug resistance is a major factor in relation to most of these diseases.

Modern medicine and treatments mean that most young people in the West grow up healthy and happy. However, there is still a lot of work to be done, especially in the developing world, to control diseases that kill.

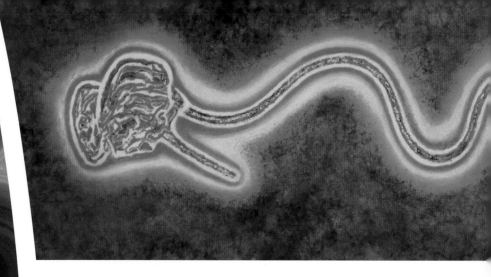

THE BUGS FIGHT BACK

Today, it is possible to treat illnesses that would have led to certain death even 20 years ago. Doctors have a whole arsenal of drugs to use against the **pathogens** that can make us sick. But the pathogens are fighting back, and drugs that once cured are becoming increasingly useless. Pathogens are microorganisms, or **microbes**, that cause disease. We often use the words *bug* or *germ*, but *pathogen* is the correct term.

HOW DRUG RESISTANCE WORKS

All living things adapt to their surroundings and find ways to survive when changes occur in their world. Pathogens are the

same. All pathogens make millions of copies of themselves every day. But not every single copy is exactly the same as the one before, and there are always small random differences known as **mutations**. Some of these mutations are able to resist the effects of drugs that would

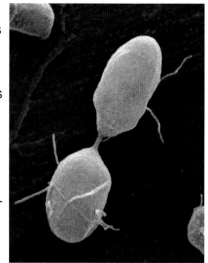

Bacteria multiply rapidly by dividing. Here, a salmonella bacterium, which can cause food poisoning, is creating two new daughter cells.

▶▶ www.who.int/topics/drug_resistance/en/

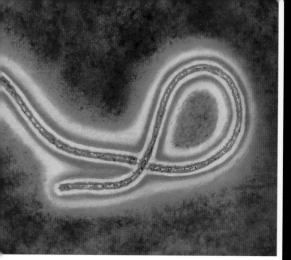

In equatorial Africa, Ebola fever is an often fatal illness that is caused by the Ebola virus (above). There have been a number of outbreaks since 1976.

normally have killed the **virus**, just because they have slightly different characteristics that are not targeted. Eventually, these mutations may outnumber those that the drugs were effective against, and when this happens, the drugs stop working. Even more worryingly, pathogens often become resistant not to just one of the drugs that is used to treat a particular disease but to all of the drugs available. That is known as multidrug resistance.

The situation is serious. Not only are new and difficult-to-treat diseases or conditions appearing, but some old foes are coming back with a vengeance. There is also the threat of terrorist attacks using once-beaten diseases, such as smallpox, in biological weapons.

A CAREER IN SCIENCE

Vanessa D'Costa is a PhD student in biochemistry at McMaster University in Ontario, Canada. She also did her undergraduate work there.

A DAY IN THE LIFE OF . . .

D'Costa is based in a lab at the McMaster Health Sciences Center, an on-campus hospital. She is currently looking into antibiotic resistance in soil and how this may provide information for predicting the ways in which resistance works in humans in clinical practice. It has been established that soil bacteria has become resistant to environmental pressures in ways that are similar to those mechanisms found in drug resistance.

THE SCIENTIST SAYS . . .

"What excites me about this work is that it may one day help us predict clinical resistance before it happens. By studying these new environmental mechanisms, we can not only develop diagnostic techniques but also establish ways to circumvent the resistance, allowing us to think one step ahead of the antibiotic-resistant bacteria."

REVENGE OF THE SUPERBUGS

There have been many stories in the news about so-called superbugs. These usually refer to a bacterium known as **MRSA** (methicillin-resistant *Staphylococcus aureus*), which has been responsible for many deaths, mostly in hospitals. But relative newcomers like MRSA are only part of the story.

A RANGE OF DANGERS

There has been a rise in diseases that medical science believed to be controllable with the right drugs. Tuberculosis (TB) is one example. TB has existed for thousands of years, but in 1943, a highly effective antibiotic called streptomycin was discovered, and other successful drugs have been developed since then. Today, strains of the bacteria that cause TB have found ways to resist these drugs. This directly threatens millions of people in many parts of the world but also has huge implications for sufferers of the HIV/AIDS virus. HIV/AIDS weakens the immune system and increases the chances of getting TB. Even worse for HIV/AIDS sufferers, despite the success of a treatment with a range of drugs known as antiretroviral therapy (**ART**), HIV is also starting to show signs of developing resistance.

Malaria is another deadly enemy that is fighting to stay ahead of the game. Incredibly, it has been responsible for more deaths throughout history than any other disease. Scientists originally believed the only solution was to wipe out the mosquito parasites that carry the disease, but this proved to be impossible. So, instead,

A female anopheles mosquito bites into human skin. The parasite responsible for malaria is carried in her saliva.

doctors focused on finding medicines to treat it. A drug called cloroquine looked like the solution, but in the 1960s, doctors realized that malaria was becoming resistant to the drug. It took only ten years for resistant strains of malaria to spread from one area of Thailand to all of Asia, Africa, and South America. Newer drugs have also shown signs of resistance, including artemisinin, which was being hailed as the magic bullet for malaria only 15 years ago.

Today, drug resistance threatens not only the health of all of us but also the notion that humans are superior to the diseases that share our planet.

INVESTIGATING THE EVIDENCE: TB AND LIFESTYLE

The investigation: Poverty is known to be associated with TB, but why is this the case? Scientists in Liverpool, U.K., have investigated the lifestyles of both TB patients and people who do not have TB.

The scientists: A team led by Professor Peter Davies, the head of the TB Research Unit at the Cardiothoracic Center in Liverpool. He is also the secretary of TB Alert, a charity that supports TB projects around the world and promotes awareness of the illness.

Collecting the evidence: The evidence was gathered by visiting people in their homes and compiling information on a wide range of lifestyle factors, including diet, travel, and living arrangements.

The conclusion: An analysis of the data showed that a diet that includes fresh fruit and vegetables and dairy products appears to have a protective effect against contracting TB or having the active form of the disease. The biggest risk factor for infection was visiting countries such as India and southern Africa. Smoking was also found to play a part in death rates from the disease, and smokers with **latent** TB were more likely to die from the illness.

CHAPTER ONE

THE WORLD OF THE MICROBE

A TEEMING MASS OF LIFE EXISTS ALL AROUND US EVERY MOMENT OF OUR LIVES, YET WE ARE BARELY AWARE THAT IT IS THERE. WE MAY LIKE TO BELIEVE THAT WE ARE IN CHARGE OF THIS PLANET, BUT MICROBES ARE THE TRUE MASTERS. SOME THRIVE IN THE MOST EXTREME TEMPERATURES THAT EARTH HAS TO OFFER. SOME NEED OXYGEN TO SURVIVE JUST AS WE DO, BUT OTHERS CAN EXIST WITHOUT IT. WELCOME TO A WORLD WHERE THE MINUSCULE RULES.

Viruses are so tiny that you need a microscope to see them. The protein shell that surrounds their genetic core attaches itself to target cells in the human body, which it then attacks.

WHAT ARE MICROBES?

Microbes are tiny organisms that we can see only with the aid of a **microscope**. They are everywhere: inside and outside our bodies, on everything we can see, and in places we cannot. They live inside and on all plants and animals.

It is estimated that the first microbial life on Earth existed around 3.5 billion years ago, compared with the "mere" 195,000 years since humans appeared.

There are four main types of microbes. They are known as bacteria, viruses, **fungi**, and **protozoans**. Bacteria are creatures made up of only one cell and are so small that 1,000 in a row could fit across the eraser on a pencil.

Viruses are even tinier. They are technically not alive at all because they cannot exist in their own right. Consisting of little more than genetic material surrounded by a coating of protein, they invade living cells and almost always cause disease. Viruses can even infect bacteria.

Fungi are a type of plant that, unlike other plants, cannot make their own food. They can be single celled or multicellular. The types of fungi we know best are mushrooms, **yeasts**, and **molds**, but around one half are microscopic varieties that can cause disease in humans. Other types can help us and are used in food preparation or the production of certain medicines.

Protozoans are one-celled creatures that may be parasites and that can cause disease in humans. Malaria is caused by a protozoan parasite.

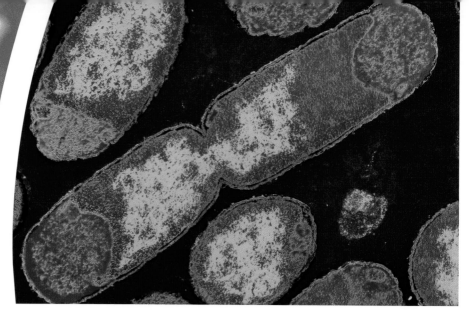

E. coli, seen here dividing and multiplying, is a bacterium that normally lives in our gut. It can be picked up accidentally, especially if we do not wash our hands properly, and may cause health problems.

SHARING THE WORLD

The overwhelming majority of the microbes on our planet either live alongside us in harmony or work actively for us in some beneficial way. Only a tiny fraction—about one percent—are harmful.

Around 100,000 billion bacteria are living on and inside your body right now. In fact, you are made up of more microbial cells than human ones. The gut alone is home to about 2.2 lbs. (1kg) of bacteria—more than the total number of people who have ever lived on the planet. Most of these microbes are "friendly." In other words, they work to protect us against other more harmful organisms. In our stomachs, they play a very important role. They break down food and help us digest it so that we can get all of the **nutrients** we need to stay healthy. The bacteria that work for us are called **commensals**.

BACTERIA AND VIRUSES

The bacteria that harm us are in the minority and are known as pathogenic bacteria. We may breathe them in or get them from direct contact. Or we may eat them if we do not cook or wash certain foods properly. Bacteria that normally live inside us without provoking trouble can also cause severe health problems if we accidentally ingest them. Bacteria can lead to various problems in different parts of the human body. Streptococcus pneumonia affects the lungs, but it is also responsible for ear infections. Some bacteria may be harmful to humans but not to plants and animals, and vice versa.

Viruses are even harder to fight than bacteria, because they do not live independently. They need to hijack other living cells in order to survive. You will probably have made a home for a rhinovirus hundreds of times—this is the virus that is responsible for the common cold.

There are many different types of rhinoviruses, which is why you can get one cold right after another.

A CAREER IN SCIENCE

Richard James is a professor of microbiology and the director of the Centre for Healthcare Associated Infections at the University of Nottingham in the U.K. While studying for his PhD in microbiology at Middlesex Hospital Medical School, he researched the bacterium E. coli. His focus now is on developing new antibiotics that are active against hospital superbugs such as MRSA and developing rapid diagnostic techniques to identify them.

A DAY IN THE LIFE . . .

Professor James directs other researchers in laboratory work, where they grow bacteria, clone and sequence genes, and look at the potential of antibiotics for killing bacteria. The university has recently set up a facility for whole **genome** sequencing so that, when a patient has a very serious infection, they can isolate the bacteria and determine its complete genome sequence in order to help understand how it is capable of causing such infections. This is the first step in developing better diagnostics to rapidly identify such bacteria in other patients and new antibiotics to be able to treat patients.

A SCIENTIST SAYS . . .

"I enjoy being able to discuss the results being generated by the researchers in my laboratory. Giving live media interviews, such as on the BBC news, is a bit scary but also fun."

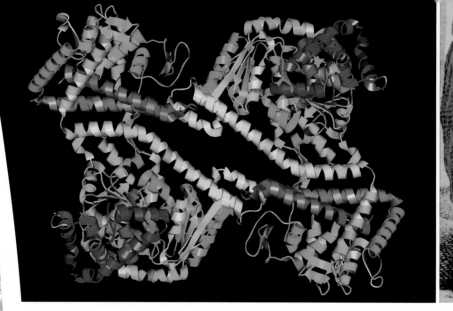

This is a computer model of the structure of a protein from a TB bacterium. By studying its structure, scientists can find out how quickly the bacterium is mutating.

EVOLUTION OVER TIME

Drug resistance is **evolution** in action. All living things need to adapt to the environment in which they live—even humans. Over time, we may evolve certain genetic traits that can protect us against illnesses. For example, in areas where a disease such as malaria is rife, a minority of people may become **resistant** to certain strains. But in the human world, this is a very slow process that takes many generations to occur, if it happens at all. Genes have to be passed on from parent to child, with around 25 years on average in between.

Evolution is a much faster process when it comes to microbes. One bacterial cell can become two in only 15 minutes, two can become four in 30 minutes, and so on. If they did not have to cope with any environmental limitations, such as starvation and other microbes, microbes could cover the surface of Earth in almost no time.

All forms of microbes are able to develop resistance to drugs that are designed to kill them. This process of fighting back is known as selective pressure. It always involves genetic changes—for example, by sharing or acquiring new genetic material.

▶ ▶ www.sdnhm.org/exhibits/epidemic/naturalhistory.html

The bacterium that caused the Great Plague in Great Britain in 1665 traveled throughout Asia, the Middle East, and other parts of Europe.

GLOBAL MOVEMENT

Bacteria do not need a long-distance flight on an airplane to move across the world, although the increase in global travel does help them hitch a ride. Even more worryingly, scientists have recently discovered that microbes are not only capable of picking up mutations from their own genetic families. It seems that they can swap and pick them up from other microbes, too. This is a global gene pool or, as some scientists have put it, a type of genetic lending library. Pathogens can pick up new traits that help them survive. This means that they can find ways to resist drugs designed to beat them.

INVESTIGATING THE EVIDENCE: HOW TO BEAT TB

The investigation: A team of scientists looked at the mechanisms of the mycobacterium responsible for TB, which is increasingly resistant to drugs.

The scientists: A team led by Professor Johnjoe McFadden of the School of Biomedical and Molecular Sciences at Surrey University, U.K. The team liaised with other bodies, including the Biotechnology and Biological Sciences Research Council (BBSRC) and the Health Protection Agency in the U.K.

Collecting the evidence: McFadden and his team used computer modeling to analyze the paths used by the latent, or "sleeping," form of the disease. People with latent TB can go on to develop the active illness and become sick. Even while the disease is active and causing symptoms, latent bacteria remain in the body.

The conclusion: Growing cultures of the latent bacteria in a lab takes a long time and does not allow scientists to analyze it in the human body. Computer modeling has allowed them to build up a picture of mechanisms that the bacteria use, and this will ultimately help find drugs that can target them more accurately.

CHAPTER TWO

DEVELOPMENT OF ANTIBIOTICS

ANTIBIOTICS HAVE BEEN DESCRIBED AS THE SINGLE MOST IMPORTANT DISCOVERY IN THE HISTORY OF MEDICINE. THEY HAVE REVOLUTIONIZED HEALTH CARE AROUND THE WORLD. BUT THEY HAVE ALSO CREATED NEW PROBLEMS IN WAYS THAT WERE NEVER FULLY ANTICIPATED BY SCIENTISTS.

HOW THEY WORK

Bacteria and fungi protect themselves from other microbes by producing substances that are poisonous to their enemies. These substances are antibiotics. Naturally occurring antibiotics existed on Earth about three billion years before humans.

Almost all of us have taken a drug form of an antibiotic at some point in our lives. Antibiotics are prescribed for bacterial infections in any part of the body but most commonly the throat, ears, and **respiratory system**.

No antibiotic is capable of wiping out all of the harmful bugs in one fell swoop. Antibiotics work by killing off the weakest bugs first—including some that have not been making you sick—and leaving behind stronger

and resistant bacteria. If you do not take the full course of an antibiotic, you leave behind the strongest bacteria, and this can lead to them developing resistance to the original drug.

Today, there are more than 150 varieties of antibiotics on the market. In many countries, antibiotics are available only by prescription from a doctor. However, in other parts of the world, they can easily be bought over the counter. It is also possible to buy antibiotics from the Internet. This means that many people are taking them without any input or advice from a doctor.

A scientist inoculates a series of culture medium plates with bacteria as part of research into new forms of antibiotics.

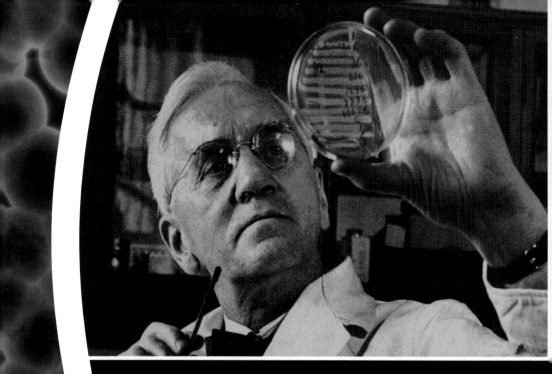

Alexander Fleming (1881–1955) was a biologist and pharmacologist at St. Mary's Hospital in London. He received a Nobel Prize along with Ernst Chain and Howard Florey for their work on penicillin.

THE DISCOVERY OF ANTIBIOTICS

A Dutch merchant named Anton van Leeuwenhoek (1632–1723) was the first person to see bacteria using his homemade microscope. But it was not until the mid-1800s that scientists agreed that these microbes could be responsible for disease. This led to the question of whether some bacteria could cure as well as kill. In 1877, Louis Pasteur, a French chemist and **microbiologist**, made a major breakthrough when he discovered that anthrax, a highly infectious bacterial disease, could be cured in animals by injecting them with soil bacteria. Other developments followed over the next few decades, but no one could find a way to make a medicine from the bacteria that was not harmful to humans.

Then, in 1928, British scientist Alexander Fleming made a chance discovery that changed the history of medicine. Returning to his laboratory after the weekend, he discovered that some scientific plates containing the staphylococcus bacteria had become moldy. The surprising part was that some of the bacteria were dead. Fleming realized that the fungus growing on the plates was creating a substance that was poisonous to the bacteria. He called the substance *penicillin*.

Unfortunately, Fleming could not find a way to extract the penicillin and turn it into a meaningful treatment. By 1941, scientists Howard Florey and Ernst Chain managed to grow enough penicillin to treat a policeman with a life-threatening illness. They injected him with penicillin, and his recovery was at first almost miraculous. However, they did not have a big enough dose to stop the infection from returning, and he died.

This is the original culture plate of the fungus *Penicillium notatum* made by Alexander Fleming at St. Mary's Hospital in 1928.

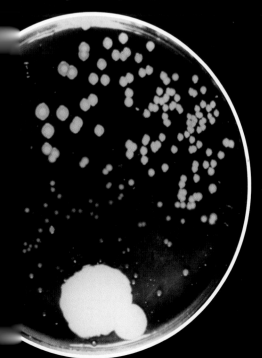

INVESTIGATING THE EVIDENCE: MICROBES AND DRUG RESISTANCE

The investigation: A team is carrying out research into patterns of drug resistance in various microbes, including bacteria, viruses, fungi, and parasites such as malaria-transmitting mosquitoes. They are analyzing new drug resistance and tracking the increase or decrease in established resistances.

The scientists: Dr. Berit Müller-Pebody of the Department of Healthcare Associated Infections and Antimicrobial Resistance's Centre for Infections at the Health Protection Agency (HPA) in the U.K., along with many other departments of the HPA and outside hospitals, laboratories, and research facilities.

Collecting the evidence: Information is taken from a huge database called LabBase that contains reports of all microorganisms retrieved from patients in almost 400 hospitals and laboratories in England and Wales.

The conclusion: Infection control strategies (such as isolating certain infected patients) have resulted in a leveling off of MRSA infections. But new resistances are being discovered in which traditional medicines have been effective, and resistance has also been found in antivirals and antifungals.

THE GOLDEN AGE OF ANTIBIOTICS

As better methods of production were found, the so-called "miracle drug" penicillin gradually became available to the mass market. For the first time in history, humans were able to claim superiority over the microbial world. However, this did not happen overnight.

THE COCOANUT GROVE FIRE

After Howard Florey and Ernst Chain's successes were reported in the medical press, scientists for the U.S. military began working in secret to try to produce the drug to treat wounded soldiers. On November 28, 1942, a fire broke out at a popular nightclub in Boston, Massachusetts, called Cocoanut Grove. Inadequate safety provisions and overcrowding—more than twice as many people were packed into the club than was allowed by law—meant that within only 15 minutes the building was an inferno. In total, 492 people died, and the lives of another 200 hung in the balance.

One of the biggest dangers for burn victims is infection. The military realized that it was time to test the new drug, and many lives were saved. But it was not until the following year that penicillin hit the news.

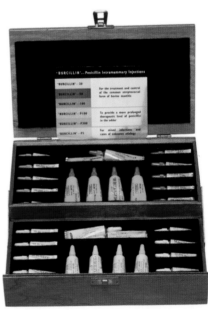

Tubes of penicillin were easily transportable to wherever they were needed.

GOING PUBLIC

A father whose baby daughter was dying of a staphylococcal blood infection contacted a major U.S. newspaper to beg for help. The editor sensed a good story and publicly challenged the group that controlled the still small supply of the drug to provide the penicillin. A car owned by the newspaper helped deliver the drug amid huge fanfare. The baby girl lived, the national press picked up the story, and before long, heartfelt pleas were pouring in from all across the country for access to the drug. By 1952, it became available on prescription in the U.K. and U.S. Before long, around two million pounds (907,000kg) of penicillin were being produced each year in the United States alone.

These women are working on a production line for pencillin in Liverpool, U.K., in 1954.

INVESTIGATING THE EVIDENCE: ANTIBIOTICS IN HISTORY

The investigation: Could a susbtance from soil called streptomycin kill the bacterium responsible for tuberculosis?

The scientists: Dr. Selman A. Waksman (1888–1973) of Rutgers University, New Jersey, and his team of students had isolated streptomycin from soil brought in by a local farmer. Waksman's student Albert Schatz (1922–2005) is believed to have done most of the work behind the discovery.

Collecting the evidence: Waksman and Schatz believed that streptomycin was active against TB, but they did not have the means to test their theory. They supplied the Mayo Clinic, based in Rochester, Minnesota, with the substance to test it, first on guinea pigs and then on human patients.

The conclusion: Streptomycin was found to be a powerful drug against the bacterium that causes TB and a range of other diseases. The drug made a huge profit for the company that developed it, but within a short span of time it became apparent that bacterium could quickly develop resistance.

Antibiotic eye drops were successfully used on a mass scale against the eye infection trachoma, which affected up to 400 million people worldwide.

A WAVE OF OPTIMISM

Over the next few decades, other types of antibiotics were discovered, such as chloramphenicol, which is still in use today. Researchers also began to look beyond naturally occurring antibiotics and found ways to make synthetic versions of these lifesaving medicines in the laboratory.

PREVENTION RATHER THAN CURE

There were other major breakthroughs happening in medicine during this period. For the first time, bodies such as WHO, founded in 1948, began to look at not only treating disease on a large scale but also at how to prevent it in the first place. Mass health programs were launched, including one targeting a tropical infection called yaws, which attacks the skin, bones, and joints. Penicillin virtually eradicated the disease in Asia for a time.

Mass vaccination programs were put in place against TB, and leprosy also became widely treatable for the first time. There was great hope about wiping out malaria, too, thanks to a new drug called choloroquine and spraying mosquitoes with the chemical **DDT**.

Doctors began to imagine a time when all infectious diseases could be conquered. In 1969, William H. Stewart, the U.S. Surgeon General, made a bold statement to Congress: "The time has come to close the book on infectious disease."

But it was a false optimism. Even in the earliest days of antibiotics, there were warning voices about taking drugs for granted and improperly using them. Alexander Fleming himself told *The New York Times*: "The greatest possible evil in self-medication is the use of too small doses so that instead of clearing up infection, the microbes are educated to resist penicillin and a host of penicillin-fast organisms." It would be a long time before the world would heed that warning.

Today, synthetic versions of many antibiotics can be manufactured quickly and easily.

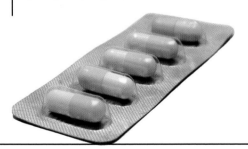

INVESTIGATING THE EVIDENCE: RESISTANCE PATTERNS

The investigation: Scientists wanted to find out exactly how large the environmental level of antibiotic resistance is in locations with both high and low human activity.

The scientists: Dr. Mirva Drobni, a molecular biologist working on antibiotic resistance in the Department of Medical Sciences/Infectious Diseases at Uppsala University, Sweden, together with Professor Bjørn Olsen, also of Uppsala University.

Collecting the evidence: The team looked at the environmental dissemination of bacterial antibiotic resistance that has a human source. They used cotton swabs to collect fecal samples from birds in different locations. The bacterial material was then analyzed in a laboratory, and the scientists looked at which antibiotics the birds were resistant to. With those that showed resistance, the team then discovered which genes may be involved in the process.

The conclusion: The scientists found that bacteria carried by birds in close proximity to human activity tend to display the same resistance patterns and genetic variants as are found in human clinical samples in that region. Studies like this are important for understanding the mechanisms underlying bacterial resistance.

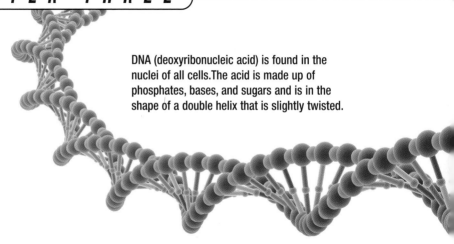

CHAPTER THREE

DNA (deoxyribonucleic acid) is found in the nuclei of all cells. The acid is made up of phosphates, bases, and sugars and is in the shape of a double helix that is slightly twisted.

MICROBES FIGHT BACK

ONLY A FEW YEARS AFTER THE FIRST USE OF PENICILLIN, SCIENTISTS AT ONE LONDON HOSPITAL DISCOVERED THAT 14 PERCENT OF STRAINS WERE ALREADY RESISTANT TO ANTIBIOTICS. BY 1946, IN THE SAME HOSPITAL, RESISTANCE WAS AS HIGH AS 59 PERCENT.

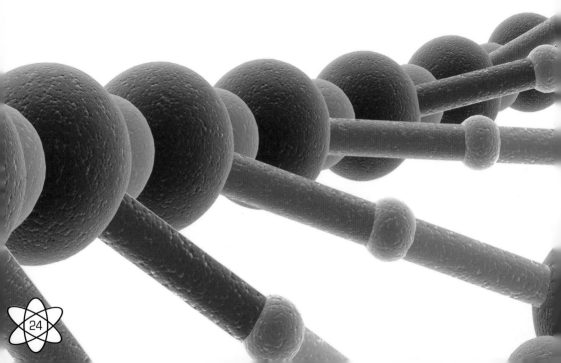

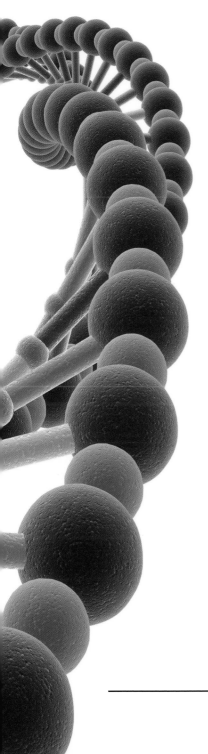

BACTERIAL MUTATION

Bacteria mutate to resist environmental threats, such as medicines, in three ways. First, they may spontaneously mutate. This means that the **DNA**—the genetic material that determines all of the characteristics of the bacteria—changes on its own. Second, a bacterium may pick up DNA from another bacterium in a mutation process called transformation. The third and most unpredictable type of mutation, however, is when resistance is acquired from a small circle of DNA known as a **plasmid**. Plasmids multiply within bacteria and can move between different species, causing resistance to multiple drug therapies. They can be seen only with very powerful machines called electron microscopes.

VIRAL MUTATION

It is not only bacteria that mutate and learn how to evade the antibiotics or synthetic drugs that are designed to kill them. Viruses have only one purpose: to reproduce. Genetic mutations usually occur by accident as a virus makes copies of itself. These can make it more resistant to protective mechanisms such as antibodies. As for other much larger microbes, the *Plasmodium falciparum* parasite that causes malaria has a highly complex genome, or collection of genes. Its ability to adapt and "hide" from the body's immune system has made it very diffcult to treat, especially because it can mutate to resist the drugs targeting it.

THE MISUSE OF ANTIBIOTICS

Although antibiotics were thought to be a savior of humankind, they were taken for granted and have been used in the wrong way for decades. Now their efficiency is seriously threatened, and we face the real prospect of a return to the days before their discovery.

RESISTANCE

The precise mechanisms of how pathogens become resistant are not clear.

In the 1980s, medical research turned its focus to other types of drug development, and there was little work being carried out on new antibiotics. Resistant strains of microbes were developing all the time, but the attitude prevailed that, if needed, there were always other antibiotics available. Today, there is resistance to almost all forms of antibiotics. Many doctors say that

In many countries, antibiotics can be bought over the counter, without a prescription.

patient expectation is one major factor. They report that many people come into their offices with symptoms of a viral infection such as a cold, sore throat, or earache and demand antibiotics to clear it up. If someone will not take no for an answer, it is often easier for the doctor to write a prescription. However, this causes more harm than good. The medicine will not play any role in the person getting better, because his or her body will fight off the bug by itself, but the patient is left with the impression that the drug has done its job.

Even when antibiotics are prescribed as they should be, if they are not taken properly, we as consumers are giving resistant strains a helping hand. The patient usually starts to feel better before the drug has been able to target all of the relevant bacteria, and this leaves behind resistant microbes that are then passed on within a community. It has been estimated that more than one half of the antibiotics used worldwide have been privately bought, and one half of those are typically used for only one day's treatment. The consequences are serious. Antibiotic resistant strains of just one bacteria, *Staphylococcus aureus*, have increased by eight percent in one year.

Today, it is increasingly easy for people to order prescription drugs over the Internet.

A CAREER IN SCIENCE

Dr. Alan Johnson is a clinical scientist—a specialist who does research and advises other scientists on the approach to a treatment that is most likely to be successful. Dr. Johnson's first degree was in biological science, and his interest in how microbes cause disease led him to specialize in medical microbiology. He is now the head of the antimicrobial resistance section of the Health Protection Agency in the U.K.

A DAY IN THE LIFE OF . . .

In his earlier career, Dr. Johnson was lab based, but now he works mostly at a computer, collecting and analyzing data. He is currently involved in studying a number of antibiotic-resistant bacteria, including MRSA. He is especially interested in how MRSA can cause bloodstream infections in children. Occasionally, Dr. Johnson gives talks about his findings, both in the U.K. and other countries.

A SCIENTIST SAYS . . .

"For me, the best thing about being a scientist is that I get to spend each day doing something I enjoy, and I actually get paid for it. Also, working in the medical field means that we can, hopefully, help improve the well-being of patients."

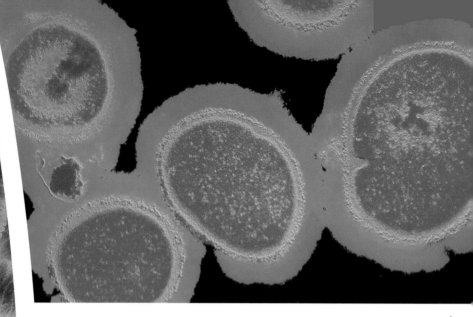

This color magnification shows a cluster of MRSA bacteria dividing. This potentially deadly bug is common in hospitals, infecting the wounds of patients.

GETTING SICK IN THE HOSPITAL

Hospitals have become a major focus for the problem of antibiotic resistance. In many countries, the media has highlighted this aspect of the issue more than any other. So why are hospitals targeted by the so-called superbugs?

FIGHTING A SUPERBUG

Superbug is a term that is normally used to refer to a bacterium known as methicillin-resistant *Staphylococcus aureus*, or MRSA. It is a pathogen that is not only resistant to methicillin but to all of the other common antibiotics that once treated it, such as penicillin, flucloxacillin, and cephalosporin. It is even showing signs of becoming resistant to vancomycin—the drug of last resort.

Hospitals are a prime target for the development of resistant strains of microbes. After all, they are places where there are many people in close contact with one another. Anywhere that humans are in confined proximity gives pathogens the opportunity to spread quickly. By their very nature, hospitals contain many different bugs, but this is not as straightforward an explanation as you might expect. Although it is easy to suppose that, because there

It is vital that everyone who comes into contact with patients thoroughly washes their hands.

are many sick people, there are more bacteria, it is actually hospital visitors who are believed to be the prime carriers of microbes.

However, people in hospitals are more vulnerable and likely to pick up opportunistic pathogens for several reasons. They may have wounds from surgery or other procedures, and these provide inviting entry points. Patients are more likely to be elderly and frail or simply in a state when their natural **immunity**—the ability to naturally fight off bugs—is at a lower level than usual. Doctors are even finding that with certain cancers, it is not the disease that ultimately kills someone but the fact that the **chemotherapy** has left the patient open to ordinary infections.

INVESTIGATING THE EVIDENCE: PREVENTING MRSA

The investigation: Scientists wanted to find out if it was possible to develop a vaccine to prevent MRSA infections and to establish why infections recur in 25 percent of cases, when people are usually immune to getting an infection once they have had it.

The scientists: Professor Gerald Pier, Dr. Tomas Maira-Litran, Dr. Jean Lee, and Dr. David Skurnik, all of Harvard Medical School in Boston, Massachusetts.

Collecting the evidence: The team identified a molecule on the surface of the MRSA bacterial cells that can be purified and injected into mice. This allowed them to see, using blood tests, if the process caused the animals to make protective antibodies. If so, the antibodies are capable of killing the MRSA bacterial cells. This means that the mice would not get an MRSA infection.

The conclusion: The team discovered that they must chemically change the surface molecule in the lab in order to make it capable of inducing antibodies that kill MRSA bacteria and protect against infection. Good results so far have set the stage for making and testing the vaccine in humans and animals.

CHAPTER FOUR

RESISTANCE AND THE ENVIRONMENT

IT IS NOT ONLY THE HUMAN CONSUMPTION OF ANTIBIOTICS THAT HAS LED TO THE DEVELOPMENT OF RESISTANCE. ANTIBIOTICS HAVE ALSO BEEN HEAVILY USED IN FARMING, AND THIS HAS RESULTED IN MAJOR IMPLICATIONS FOR HUMAN HEALTH.

TREATING ANIMALS FOR PRODUCTIVITY

Animals are prey to a range of bacterial infections just like humans, and farmers soon realized that the results in treating certain animal diseases with drugs were impressive. However, since the 1950s, the drugs have been used not only to cure infections but also to promote animal growth. Today, low doses are still added to the feed given to livestock. The idea is that the drugs prevent low-

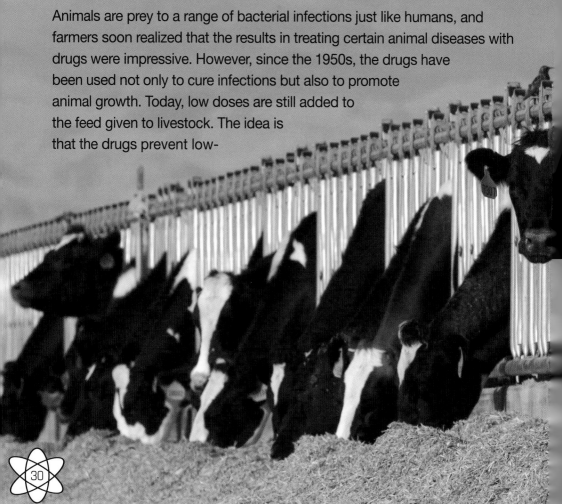

level diseases in the animals. And using antibiotics in livestock also means that animals can be reared more intensively, with stocks kept packed together in close proximity without infections spreading quickly.

In 1969, a committee of scientists warned the world of the "real and potential danger" that overuse of antibiotics in animals would help speed up the rate at which bacteria learned to resist drugs. Some antibiotics have even been banned in Europe and the United States. But, despite this, the combined use for **therapeutic** and growth purposes has continued to increase, according to the U.S. pressure group The Pew Campaign on Human Health and Industrial Farming, which reports that animal production accounts for 70 percent of the antibiotics used in the U.S. Experts believe that this is helping add to the "resistance pool" of microbes, releasing them into the environment, where they can grow and become stronger.

Antibiotics are usually added to the feed of animals such as cattle, pigs, sheep, and chickens.

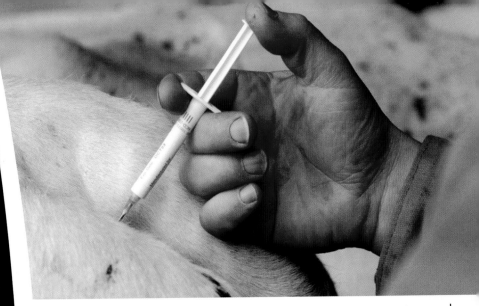

Farmers routinely ask vets to inject cattle with antibiotics in order to prevent illness and increase profitability. However, this results in drug-resistant germs being passed on to humans.

THE ENVIRONMENTAL CONNECTION

Most animal bacteria cannot survive in humans and therefore do not present a health threat. However, certain microbes are capable of causing severe and even deadly stomach upsets. There is increasing evidence that resistant forms of these have come about because of the way in which antibiotics have been used in farming. Salmonella is a bacterium that lives in the guts of animals, birds, and humans, but if it is accidentally eaten, the infection can be spread by excreted bacteria long after all the symptoms have cleared up. Campylobacter is another pathogen that can be dangerous to humans, and it causes similar symptoms. Both can lead to fatal conditions such as septicemia, a type of blood poisoning. Another dangerous microbe that can live in both humans and animals is *Escherida coli*, or E. coli, which can cause kidney damage and death.

HAZARDOUS FOOD

Food poisoning affects an estimated 40 million people worldwide every year, according to WHO. Microbiologists believe that the use of antibiotics in farming is a major contributing factor to the

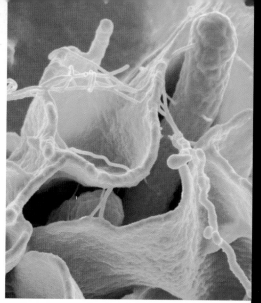

Here, *Salmonella typhimurium* bacteria (green) invade human cells.

number of food poisoning cases worldwide. A study by scientists at the University of Georgia found that bacteria with resistance to common antibiotics was high even in chickens raised without the drugs. It is possible that this resistance is actually being carried in the genes from the birds' parents.

There have been many calls for a ban on antibiotic use for growth promotion. Some experts say that without antibiotics in farming, humans will be under a bigger threat from disease-causing microbes. But it seems clear that the overuse of antibiotics is causing a rise in infections that may not respond to the only weapons we have left.

A CAREER IN SCIENCE

Dr. Arthur Thompson is the group leader of salmonella molecular microbiology at the Institute of Food Research (IFR) in Norwich, U.K. He has been at the IFR since 1996 and has set up state-of-the-art facilities to study bacterial genes involved in infection. He is now concentrating on researching the salmonella bacteria.

A DAY IN THE LIFE OF . . .

Dr. Thompson and his colleagues are working to determine the genetic programming that causes salmonella to become virulent. They want to establish which nutrients salmonella needs for infection. This work has led to a patent for a vaccine. A typical day is spent drafting publications and proposals for further research as well as advising other scientists.

THE SCIENTIST SAYS . . .

"It's exciting and rewarding to discover new things. This for me is the 'get out of bed' factor! Over the past decade or so, pathogenic salmonella strains have started to become resistant to multiple antibiotics in animals and humans, which constitutes a major future threat to animal and human health. Hence, there is a need to continually develop novel therapeutic strategies."

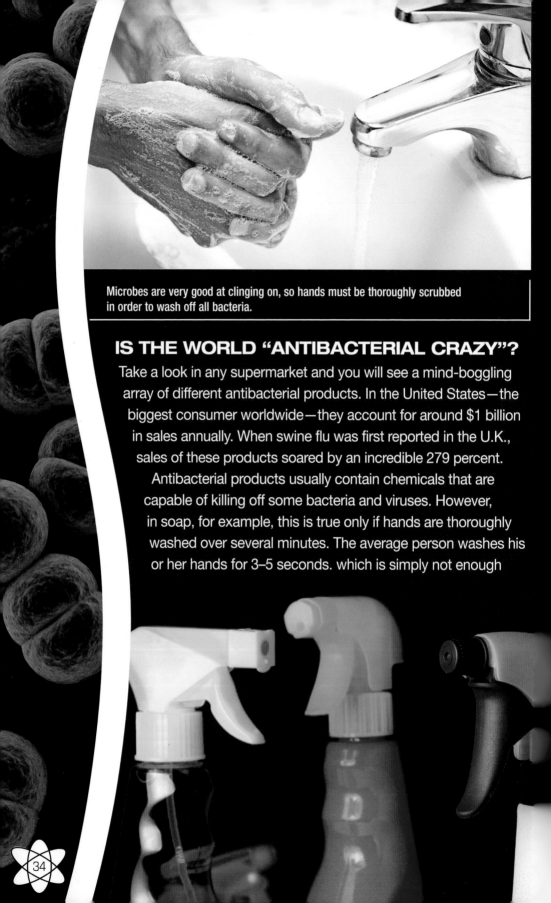

Microbes are very good at clinging on, so hands must be thoroughly scrubbed in order to wash off all bacteria.

IS THE WORLD "ANTIBACTERIAL CRAZY"?

Take a look in any supermarket and you will see a mind-boggling array of different antibacterial products. In the United States—the biggest consumer worldwide—they account for around $1 billion in sales annually. When swine flu was first reported in the U.K., sales of these products soared by an incredible 279 percent. Antibacterial products usually contain chemicals that are capable of killing off some bacteria and viruses. However, in soap, for example, this is true only if hands are thoroughly washed over several minutes. The average person washes his or her hands for 3–5 seconds. which is simply not enough time. While a few of the microbes are washed off, plenty remain.

EVERYDAY USE

Studies show that seven percent of a particular listeria bacteria that causes severe stomach upsets is now resistant to the ammonia compounds found in most cleaning products. Recently, researchers in Japan discovered that the bacteria responsible for a particular type of MRSA quickly evolved a resistance not only to antibacterial chemicals but also to several antibiotics. This means that, in effect, people are helping the rise of resistant microbes by everyday actions involving household products.

Antibacterial products usually contain chemicals such as triclosan, triclocarban, and quaternary ammonium compounds, which are capable of killing off some bacteria and viruses.

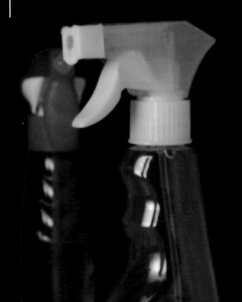

INVESTIGATING THE EVIDENCE: THE DANGERS OF USA600

The investigation: The goal was to determine whether a certain strain of MRSA called USA600 is more dangerous than others for patients infected with it.

The scientists: Team leader Carol Moore from the Henry Ford Hospital Division of Infectious Diseases in Detroit, Michigan, and Dr. Marcus Zervos, Mary Beth Perri, Susan Donabedian, Nadia Haque, Dr. Paola Osaki-Kiyan, Dr. Anne Chen, and Mei Lu.

Collecting the evidence: The team collected information about patients and the infection, especially whether or not the patients lived or died from the infection and how they were treated. The bacteria causing the infection were also collected and analyzed in a microbiology laboratory.

The conclusion: Patients who get infected with this strain of MRSA died five times more often than those infected with other strains. The study found that 50 percent of the patients infected with the strain died within 30 days compared to 11 percent of patients infected with other MRSA strains. But the patients who got infected with the USA600 strain tended to be older and sicker, which complicates the statistics. The USA600 strain was found to be more resistant to antibiotics, such as vancomycin, usually used to treat MRSA.

CHAPTER FIVE

OLD ENEMIES, NEW INVADERS

IT IS ONE OF THE OLDEST KNOWN DISEASES, BUT THERE WAS A TIME IN THE 1900s WHEN EVERYONE BELIEVED THAT TUBERCULOSIS COULD BE BEATEN. SO WHY IS TB STILL KILLING TWO MILLION PEOPLE WORLDWIDE EVERY YEAR?

BATTLING TB

The earliest documented case of TB was discovered in the spine of an Iron Age man who died in around 300 B.C. TB remained a major global killer until the mid-1900s, when an effective antibiotic—streptomycin—was discovered. This, coupled with a vaccination known as BCG (Bacillus Calmette-Guérin), meant that the disease was controllable for the first time.

Since 1988, TB has been on the increase, and in 1993, WHO declared it a global emergency. Today, there are around nine million active cases worldwide—one third of the world's population.

TB is caused by the bacterium *Mycobacterium tuberculosis*, which gets into the lungs and **lymphatic system**. Over time, it can spread to other parts of the body and cause multiple symptoms. Even if you do not get sick, you can carry it in a latent form. With the right combination of relatively cheap antibiotics taken over a period of time, TB is often completely curable.

Multidrug-resistant tuberculosis is known as **MDR-TB**, and it has now been reported in 100 different countries or territories. The only drugs that can tackle it are expensive and dangerous and have to be used for a longer period of time. TB also forms a deadly alliance with HIV/AIDS, because HIV/AIDS attacks the body's natural defenses and allows TB to become active. TB can speed up the HIV/AIDS rate of **replication**, increasing the amount of HIV in a person's syste. It is still not known why this happens.

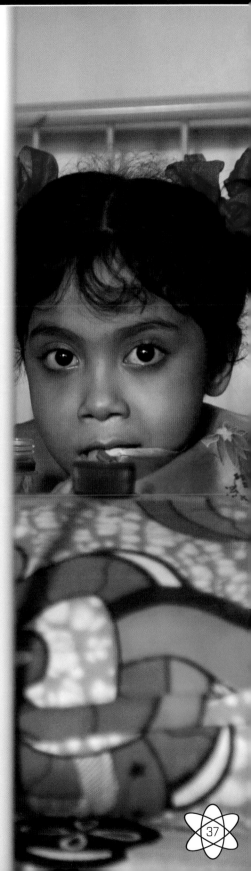

TB is rife in developing parts of the world, such as sub-Saharan Africa and Southeast Asia, where many poor and malnourished people live.

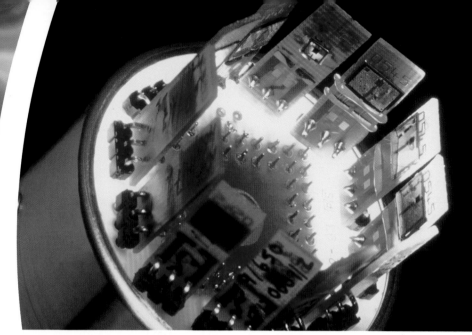

This is a close-up view of the detector head of the Neotronics Olfactory Sensing Equipment (E-Nose, see box right), which detects the contents of odors and aromas.

MRSA, SUPERBUG

MRSA stands for methicillin-resistant *Staphylococcus aureus*. The italicized part is the general name of the bacterium, and this particular strain is one that is resistant to the drug methicillin, which once treated it. *S. aureus* is a bacterium that lives on the skin and in the nose. Around 30 percent of the population carries it without it causing any problems. If, for example, you cut yourself and the wound starts to produce pus, an *S. aureus* infection is likely to be the cause. In most cases, a person's immune system is able to fight off the threat, but in the hospital, people are less able to combat the bacterium. MRSA is the most common cause of HAIs (hospital-acquired infections). In the U.S., it is estimated that one in 20 people visiting the hospital will get an HAI, and 90,000 will die each year.

MRSA

Antibiotics such as methicillin and flucloxacillin were able to beat these infections in the past. Today, the only treatment option is often an antibiotic called vancomycin, which is much

▶▶ www.amm.co.uk/files/factsabout/fa_mrsa.htm

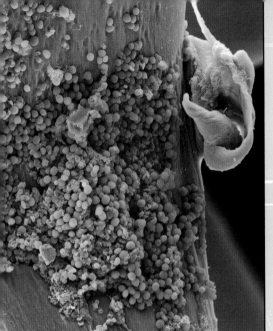

MRSA bacteria is carried around by about 30 percent of people without causing any symptoms.

more expensive and toxic to patients. Since 2004, there have been cases resistant to vancomycin—known as VRSA infections. This raises the frightening possibility of infections that we have no method of treating. Even with treatment, about 25 percent of people infected with MRSA currently die—around 5,000 people per year.

MRSA can also occur, less seriously, outside a hospital setting. So-called community-acquired MRSA, or C-MRSA, has been found in otherwise healthy people who have not recently been in the hospital or had courses of antibiotics. If caught early, it can be treated with antibiotics other than methicillin.

INVESTIGATING THE EVIDENCE: SCREENING BACTERIA

The investigation: To find a novel technique that will allow hospitals to rapidly screen for bacterial infections. Conventional pathological laboratory-based methods are flawed because they are expensive and slow, resulting in delays and poorer care for infected patients.

The scientists: Dr. Ritaban Dutta of Scensive Technologies Ltd., U.K., working with various groups of doctors from hospitals in the U.K. and India.

Collecting the evidence: The scientists looked into technology known as an electronic nose, or E-Nose, that "smells" bacteria. They wanted to find out if an E-NOSE could be used to sniff out certain bacterial infections. Six hundred patients infected with MRSA and two other bacteria were given swabs of the ear, nose, and throat to collect samples. Dr. Dutta developed an intelligent sensory system to pick up gases —or "smells"—produced by the bacteria.

The conclusion: The E-Nose was found to be successful in detecting infections in almost 100 percent of cases. It could correctly detect three strains of *Salmonella aureus* with more than 99 percent accuracy. This work has led to a further investigation into how the device can be used.

Long-distance flights are just one of the ways in which superbugs travel around the world. Whether people travel for their health or for tourism, there is a danger of infection.

EMERGING THREATS

Along with the existing threats from known enemies, new superbugs may emerge at any time as bacteria become resistant to first-line treatments. This may be partly because of the global nature of health care. People travel thousands of miles to have procedures such as cosmetic surgery in countries where they are less expensive. This can result in microbes being brought back to places where they did not previously exist. In settings such as hospitals, the microbes can quickly proliferate.

BUGS THAT TRAVEL

Hospitals in the U.S., Canada, U.K., Greece, France, China, and South America have reported a rise in a type of bacteria known as enterobacteriaceae. These bacteria are resistant to the standard antibiotic treatments used for severe infections—drugs that are called carbapenems and that are seen as the drugs of last resort.

Enterobacteriaceae live harmlessly in the guts of many people without causing any problems. The carbapenem-resistant varieties are being carried to Europe from India, Pakistan, Turkey, and other countries. They generally affect people whose immune systems are vulnerable, and they can be fatal. Because there is no real treatment for infections of this type, all hospitals can do is to be vigilant in tracking cases. Guidelines are being issued stating that rigorous infection-control procedures should be put into place if infections are identified.

Carbapenems are widely available on the Indian subcontinent, which is one of the main reasons why people's resistance to the drug has developed. The chances of picking up an infection like this in the hospital are still small, say doctors, but it is important that careful monitoring takes place so that this bug does not become as widespread and dangerous as MRSA.

Enterobacteriaceae have flagella (hairlike strands) that are used for movement.

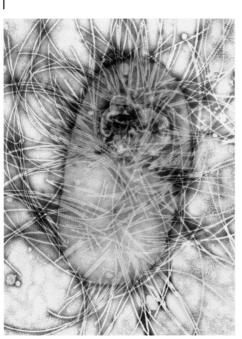

INVESTIGATING THE EVIDENCE: ANTIBIOTICS

The investigation: The goal of the research was to determine whether antibiotic resistance in environmental microbes had changed owing to increased mass production and use of antibiotics since World War II.

The scientists: Professor David Graham, University of Newcastle, U.K.; Dr. Charles Knapp, University of Newcastle (now at the University of Strathclyde); Dr. Jan Dolfing, University of Newcastle; Dr. Phillip Ehlert, Wageningen University, the Netherlands.

Collecting the evidence: The team chose to work with soils because they retain usable DNA over long periods of time. They chose soils that spanned from 1940 to the present, extracting and categorizing DNA, using molecular biological methods to count genes in each soil sample that indicated potential antibiotic resistance.

The conclusion: The scientists found that 78 percent of the genes detected were increasing over time, especially in the past 20 years. This is important because increases in genes that show resistance to four major classes of antibiotics are used to treat diseases in humans and animals.

Around 1,800 children contract the HIV/AIDS virus every day. This happens mostly in developing countries and mostly by mother-to-child transmission.

HIV/AIDS

Today, around 33 million people worldwide are infected with HIV/AIDS. Caused by HIV (human immunodeficiency virus), the disease kills or damages the body's immune system and gradually prevents it from being able to fight off infections and cancers. HIV/AIDS can be contracted in various ways, including sexual intercourse and via infected blood products, but it can also be passed from mother to child.

Since the mid-1990s, a lifesaving treatment known as antiretroviral therapy (ART) has been in existence, combining three or four different drugs that can inhibit the virus. ART, or HAART (highly active antiretroviral therapy), is expensive. It works by targeting different parts of the virus through a "cocktail" of drugs taken together.

▶ ▶ www.aidshealth.org

However, the virus is even becoming resistant to ART. HIV replicates at a very fast rate. It mostly affects CD4 cells, which are important for immunity, by damaging them and preventing them from doing their jobs while also helping the virus replicate. Mutations do not occur because the virus is finding clever ways to beat the available drugs. The consequences are not only that infected people cannot be treated but also that they are able to pass on the new highly resistant form of the virus to other people.

A CAREER IN SCIENCE

Dr. Brendan Larder is one of the world's leading experts in HIV drug resistance. He is currently the chairperson of the Response Database Initiative in the U.K., which monitors HIV resistance worldwide. He was largely responsible for discovering resistance to AZT drugs and also helped unravel the genetic basis of resistance.

A DAY IN THE LIFE OF . . .

Dr. Larder spent 20 years working in laboratories, where he studied viruses such as HIV and analyzed their responses to different drugs. He also traveled throughout Europe and the U.S.

THE SCIENTIST SAYS . . .

"The first drugs developed to treat HIV were given to patients singly (monotherapy). Drug resistance occurred in every case where a patient took only one drug. This prompted us to think that treatment might be much more effective if more than one drug was given at a time (combination therapy). The development of safe and potent HIV drugs that can be given in combination has revolutionized the HIV/AIDS treatment area. The RDI, where I work now, is important in order to identify patterns of treatment success and failure. Then using this information, developed from building computer models, we hope to enhance and improve HIV treatment ."

Pest controllers spray the pesticide DDT in a village in Madagascar. It was believed that DDT could be used to eradicate the anopheles mosquito altogether.

MALARIA

Malaria kills more people than almost any other disease. It hits the very young more than any other group, and a child dies from it somewhere around the world every 30 seconds. Resistance to the drugs used to treat it is making it even harder to cure.

In 1880, a French doctor, Charles Louis Alphonse Laveran, discovered that malaria was caused by a single-celled protozoan parasite, plasmodium, that is transmitted in the saliva of types of female mosquitoes. It can be picked up from an infected human and then passed on to someone else. It can also spread very quickly in areas where particular species of mosquitoes, mostly one called *Anopheles gambiae*, are prevalent. More than 90 percent of cases are in sub-Saharan Africa. Poor living conditions, wars, the disintegration of health services, and refugee movements all contribute to its existence.

Briefly in the last century, it was believed that wiping out the mosquito was the way forward, and a powerful chemical known as DDT was found to be an effective weapon against the parasite. Huge amounts were sprayed to kill the malarial mosquitoes. But the mosquitoes fought back. It was not long before mutations in the genes of the parasites allowed them to dodge the effects.

▶ ▶   www.who.int/topics/malaria/en

Drug therapies were tried instead, and one called cloroquine, which was first used to treat the disease in 1946, proved to be effective for many years. However, just one resistant malaria parasite was all it took for a new strain of the disease to take off.

Since the 1970s, there have been at least seven new forms of antimalarial drugs, but in each case, resistance has developed, the drug is too expensive, or it causes too many **side effects** to be a viable option. Artemisinin, originally from a Chinese herb, and its **derivatives** now have a 95 percent cure rate. WHO says that the drugs must be used in a "cocktail" with others— a little like the ART treatment for HIV/AIDS. But there are signs that resistance to artemisinins is beginning in Southeast Asia.

The parasite responsible for malaria is carried in the saliva of the female mosquito.

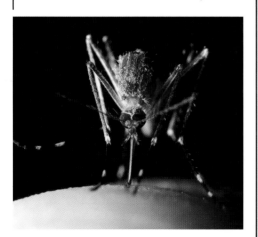

INVESTIGATING THE EVIDENCE: MALARIA

The investigation: To find out why anopheles mosquitoes are so good at transmitting malaria. The mosquitoes must survive for 10–14 days in order to do so, and most do not live that long. This means that a relatively small proportion carries the disease.

The scientists: A team led by Dr. Peter Billingsley of the School of Biological Sciences at the University of Aberdeen in Scotland, working with scientists at the university and from other research groups around the world.

Collecting the evidence: In the lab, the team maintains colonies of mosquitoes and uses them in a wide range of experiments. Collaborating scientists in the field collect the mosquitoes from different locations, using techniques that include satellite tracking systems to map movement.

The conclusion: Mosquito molecules play a vital role in transmitting malaria. By feeding antibodies to the mosquitoes, the team reduced their ability to transmit malaria. This technique makes it possible to reduce the insects' life expectancy, which further decreases its chances of transmitting malaria.

CHAPTER SIX

FINDING A SOLUTION

DRUG RESISTANCE IS A SERIOUS GLOBAL PROBLEM. IF THERE IS ANY CHANCE OF WINNING THIS BATTLE, EXPERTS MUST FIRST KNOW THEIR ENEMY. IN ORDER TO DO SO, THEY GATHER VITAL UP-TO-DATE INFORMATION ABOUT THE PATTERNS OF RESISTANCE WORLDWIDE.

NEW RESISTANCE

Just one drug-resistant microbe is all it takes for a new difficult-to-treat strain of an infectious disease to spread. In these days of cheap and easy international travel, it is only a matter of time before a strain finds its way around the world. Experts need to monitor cases of drug-resistant infections and track their progress internationally.

In 1998, an organization called the Alliance for the Prudent Use of Antibiotics (APUA) formed GAARD (Global Advisory on Antibiotic Resistance Data). They brought together surveillance projects and major organizations involved in infectious disease control, including WHO and the U.S. Centers for Disease Control (CDC).

In 2002, scientists found the first signs of resistance to an important class of drugs called quinolones in *Haemophilus influenzae*, a bacterium that causes pneumonia and meningitis (a dangerous inflammation of the brain and spinal cord). The discovery of a new resistant strain of this bacterium was a direct consequence of work by GAARD. People working in many locations around the world directly feed information to the scientists who monitor resistance. This information is used for educating the public and keeping track of the spread of resistance.

Today, EARSS (European Antimicrobial Resistance Surveillance System), a monitoring and information system on bacterial resistance, links national networks throughout countries in Europe.

LA SCIENCE A E

Virologists need to wear
full-body protective suits
when they are working
with dangerous virus
samples in a laboratory.

Laboratory technicians culture samples from patients in order to identify the types of bacteria that might be present. They grow and analyze the bacteria in petri dishes (above).

PLAYING A VITAL ROLE

Decades of the misuse of antibiotics cannot be reversed, but getting the message across about the right way to use these valuable drugs may at least help limit some of the damage in the future. And this is where we can all play our part.

TAKING ACTION

Over the past few years, there have been public information campaigns in different countries about the dangers of inappropriate antibiotic use. However, the message has still not reached enough people. Rates of antibiotic resistance have been found to be higher in southern European countries such as Greece and Spain and lowest in Scandinavian countries. In the U.S., the Food and Drug Administration (FDA) has teamed up with the CDC to create a campaign called "Get Smart: Know When Antibiotics Work." This campaign aims to educate the public about when it is best to take antibiotics.

Everyone should follow these simple rules:

- Most common infections are caused by viruses, not bacteria. Do not ask your doctor to prescribe an antibiotic unless you have a bacterial infection.
- Always take the drug in exactly the way it is presribed by the doctor. If you do not finish the course, you are killing off only the weakest bacteria and are allowing the stronger ones to flourish and fight back.
- Never take antibiotics that have been prescribed for someone else.
- Avoid using too many antibacterial products in your home. Ordinary soap and water are better than antibacterial soaps, which may increase resistance in the environment.
- Thoroughly wash your hands to curb the spread of infections.

Antibiotics may do patients more harm than good if they are taken but are not really needed.

A CAREER IN SCIENCE

Stuart Levy is a professor of molecular biology and microbiology and the director of the Center for Adaptation Genetics and Drug Resistance at Tufts University School of Medicine in Boston, Massachusetts. He is the author of the best-selling book *The Antibiotic Paradox*, now in its second edition, which was important in alerting the world to the dangers of antibiotic misuse when it was first published in 1992. In 1981, he set up the Alliance for the Prudent Use of Antibiotics (APUA).

A DAY IN THE LIFE OF . . .

Professor Levy's work is split between the Center for Adaptation Genetics and Drug Resistance at Tufts, the APUA, and a role at a drug company called Paratek Pharmaceuticals. He founded the company, and his research is key to work on new drugs and treatments for resistant pathogens. Professor Levy occasionally appears on television and in newspaper and magazine articles.

THE SCIENTIST SAYS . . .

"It is vital that we appreciate the global picture of resistance. At the APUA, our goal is to bring resources to countries so that they can do high-quality testing. We mustn't lose the 'black boxes' that are out there, particularly in African countries lacking resources."

The MRSA bacterium is usually brought into hospitals by visitors—around 30 percent of the population carries it naturally in their bodies.

FIGHTING MRSA

The superbug MRSA (see pages 28–29) is a major problem in the U.S., and recent figures from the CDC show that 90,000 deaths are caused by it every year. About one in 20 Americans will pick up a hospital-acquired infection (HAI) of this type, but states are not required by law to report the figures. One study found that up to 60 percent of these infections are resistant to the first-line antibiotics that are used to treat them. The CDC has launched a range of measures to try to curb the spread of MRSA, including awareness campaigns and case monitoring.

TAKING ACTION

In some parts of Europe, hospitals are required by law to report all cases of MRSA. Many hospitals post information reminding patients and visitors about the importance of hand washing. This is because MRSA is not only caused by a lack of hygiene on the part of doctors and nurses—it is often carried in people's bodies. However, it makes sense that having strict rules about washing hands will help cut the spread of an infection. Even the neckties that some doctors wear have

▶▶ www.mayoclinic.com/health/hand-washing/HQ00407

been found to be a potential source of infection.

If you visit someone in the hospital, you may see posters reminding visitors about the importance of hand washing. This is especially necessary for the most vulnerable patients, such as those in intensive care. Dispensers of alcohol gels, which can kill bacteria, are also positioned outside most hospital rooms, and visitors are encouraged to use them before entering.

There are alcohol-gel dispensers at the foot of many hospital beds, especially in intensive care.

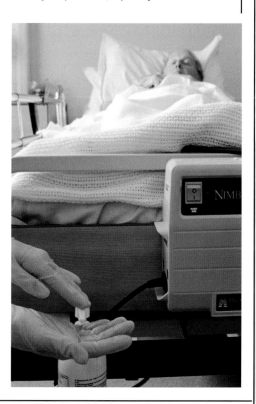

INVESTIGATING THE EVIDENCE: NEW ENZYMES

The investigation: Scientists looked at a new antibiotic called simocyclinone, which is a good target for antibacterial action.

The scientists: Professor Tony Maxwell, Marcus Edwards, Dr. David Lawson, Lesley Mitchenall, Dr. Mark Buttner, Dr. Clare Stephenson, Tung Le (all at the John Innes Centre, Norwich, U.K.), Dr. Tom Clarke (University of East Anglia, Norwich, U.K.), Dr. Adam McKay (University College London, U.K.), and Dr. Hans-Peter Fiedler (University of Tubingen, Germany).

Gathering the evidence: The team targeted an enzyme, DNA gyrase, that is essential in all bacteria. They took purified simocyclinone from soil bacteria and then made crystals that were exposed to a powerful x-ray. This revealed how the drug binds to the enzyme and showed how it works.

The conclusion: The team discovered that simocyclinone knocks out DNA gyrase by a completely new mechanism. The scientists hope this discovery will enable other scientists to develop future clinical antibiotics to exploit this mechanism.

CHAPTER SEVEN

LOOKING TO THE FUTURE

AFTER DECADES OF COMPLACENCY ABOUT THE ROLE OF MEDICINES IN FIGHTING INFECTIOUS DISEASES, SCIENCE IS LOOKING FOR NEW WAYS TO COMBAT DRUG-RESISTANT MICROBES. WITH TUBERCULOSIS (TB) AT LEAST, THERE MAY BE HOPE ON THE HORIZON FOR FUTURE TREATMENTS.

GLOBAL ACTION

In 2006, a new global effort to attack TB was announced at the World Economic Forum meeting in Davos, Switzerland. The Global Plan to Stop TB is ambitious—it wants to halve the number of yearly deaths to one million by 2015. It also aims to make available the first new drug in the past 40 years by the end of 2010, but despite current trials, this is unlikely to make the deadline. The goal is also to improve treatment programs for up to 50 million people worldwide. Funding for the program comes from charitable groups such as the U.K. Department for International Development and the U.S. Agency for International Development, as well as the governments of countries where

TB is a major health problem. Despite an increase in this funding, the plan is still short of around $1 billion.

TESTING METHODS

Currently, patients are tested for TB by a method that has been around for more than 125 years and that has a failure rate of 50 percent. It is known as the **sputum** culture. This involves producing sputum, which is any mucuslike material that can be coughed up, and then analyzing it under a microscope to look for the mycobacterium that causes TB. According to WHO, only two percent of MDR-TB (multidrug-resistant TB) cases worldwide are diagnosed and treated appropriately. There are many new tests under development.

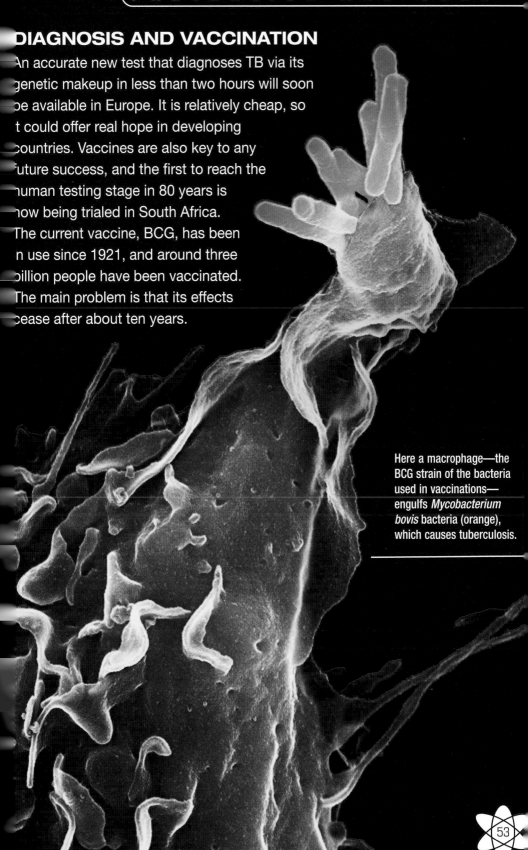

DIAGNOSIS AND VACCINATION

An accurate new test that diagnoses TB via its genetic makeup in less than two hours will soon be available in Europe. It is relatively cheap, so it could offer real hope in developing countries. Vaccines are also key to any future success, and the first to reach the human testing stage in 80 years is now being trialed in South Africa. The current vaccine, BCG, has been in use since 1921, and around three billion people have been vaccinated. The main problem is that its effects cease after about ten years.

Here a macrophage—the BCG strain of the bacteria used in vaccinations— engulfs *Mycobacterium bovis* bacteria (orange), which causes tuberculosis.

Here, freeze-dried bovine vaccinations are being examined and stored in an animal laboratory. The vaccinations can be stored for a long time without deteriorating.

RESISTANCE AND HIV/AIDS

In 2005, HIV/AIDS reached a record figure of 40 million people worldwide. It has now overtaken the Black Death of the 1300s as the worst pandemic in human history. More than 60 percent of the total number of infected people live in sub-Saharan Africa, and in some countries there, it has brought life expectancy down to only 34 years of age.

One of the key goals in fighting HIV/AIDS is the development of an effective vaccine. Over the past 20 years, there have been several dozen projects around the world working on vaccines, and more money has been spent on this than on any other vaccine research in medical history. A vaccine for the virus remains elusive, and some scientists doubt that one will be found because of the virus's ability to replicate.

OLD AND NEW APPROACHES

Many different approaches are being taken, including those based on gene therapy, where faulty or damaged genes are replaced with healthy ones. The International AIDS Vaccine Initiative (IAVI) is a nonprofit organization that promotes research around the world. It claims that a record number of people are currently involved in clinical trials. At present, there are 18 drugs in 40 different strengths in Europe that are approved for HIV/AIDS treatment. Combinations of these drugs, in highly active antiretroviral therapy (HAART), has been an effective therapy for the past 15 years, albeit in a drug regime that has side effects and may be difficult to handle. According to the American Pharmacists' Association (APA), up to 16 percent of patients are resistant to at least one of the antiretroviral drugs. Research over recent years has focused more on refining existing drugs than finding new ones, and there have been few brand-new medicines released onto the market.

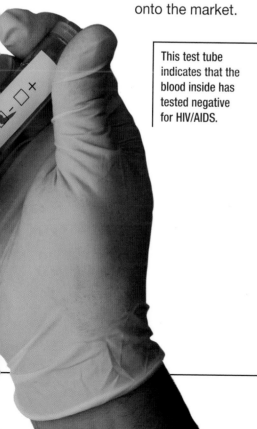

This test tube indicates that the blood inside has tested negative for HIV/AIDS.

A CAREER IN SCIENCE

Immunologist Dr. David Margolis works at the Michael Hooker Research Center at the University of North Carolina at Chapel Hill. The center is a state-of-the-art research facility but is also a clinical setting for real patients. Margolis realized while he was still at medical school that he had an interest in research, and he chose to specialize in virology. He is now involved in HIV research, looking into the molecular mechanisms of the virus in order to produce more effective treatments.

A DAY IN THE LIFE OF . . .

Dr. Margolis spends most of the week analyzing data at his computer, but he also works in the laboratory, culturing cells in incubators and observing the mechanisms of HIV at work. Because the center is also a working medical facility, patients are directly involved in trying out any new treatments.

THE SCIENTIST SAYS . . .

"The first priority is to make sure that the patients are not harmed. That's always challenging, because while two mice are always the same, two people never are. When you are better able to understand how a virus works and can use that knowledge to improve the health of people, that's very exciting."

There have been many different approaches to tackling malaria over the years, from attacking the mosquitos that carry the disease to vaccination programs and treatment.

PREVENTING MALARIA

The toll of malaria on children alone has been likened to seven packed jumbo jets crashing every single day. More than 100 years since the *Plasmodium falciparum* microbe responsible was first identified, are we any closer to finding a way to beat it?

Several malaria vaccine trials are being developed, but registration of a product is still many years away. There are more than a dozen different projects around the world working on a malaria vaccine. The biggest hope lies with artemisinin, to which the parasite has not yet become resistant. Elsewhere, a combination of two different antimalarials in a drug called Coartem has been licensed for use by the U.S. FDA with a 96 percent success rate.

There is also research being conducted into the mosquito itself and how its genetics, physiology, and **ecology** can be used to find new ways to treat, prevent, or control the disease. One example is the possibility of genetically engineering mosquitoes that would be incapable of carrying the infectious parasite. This may involve inserting genes into mosquitoes to stop the parasite from developing.

In a strange twist on the debate about antibacterial products and their role in promoting microbial resistance, studies have shown that impregnating household surfaces with a certain type of fungus may help curb the spread of the disease. The challenge now is to develop this technology into an inexpensive product.

A child in Tanzania is vaccinated against malaria.

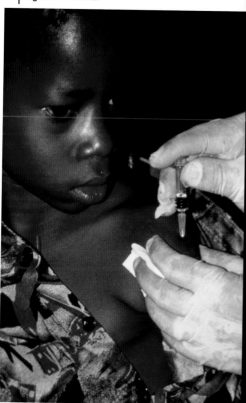

A CAREER IN SCIENCE

Pediatric parasite expert Dr. Michele Spring works at the Walter Reed Army Institute of Research in Silver Spring, Maryland. After studying parasitology, she joined the Peace Corps in West Africa, where she traveled to small villages to help combat a disease called guinea worm. She became a padiatrician with an interest in how children are affected by parasitic diseases. She is now involved in malaria vaccine research.

A DAY IN THE LIFE OF . . .

Dr Spring spends most of her time in the office or clinic, organizing studies to test malaria vaccines in volunteers. She helps give out new malaria vaccines, monitors the volunteers to see if the vaccines have any side effects, and takes blood to see how the volunteers' immune systems react to the vaccines. Sometimes, volunteers are given malaria by a mosquito bite in order to see if the vaccines protect them against the disease. Someday, Dr. Spring hopes that a vaccine tested in the clinic will be available to help children in Africa.

THE SCIENTIST SAYS . . .

"What inspires me about this research is the chance that this work may reduce the threat of malaria infection and disease from certain parts of the world and that children more susceptible to malaria can grow up healthy and strong."

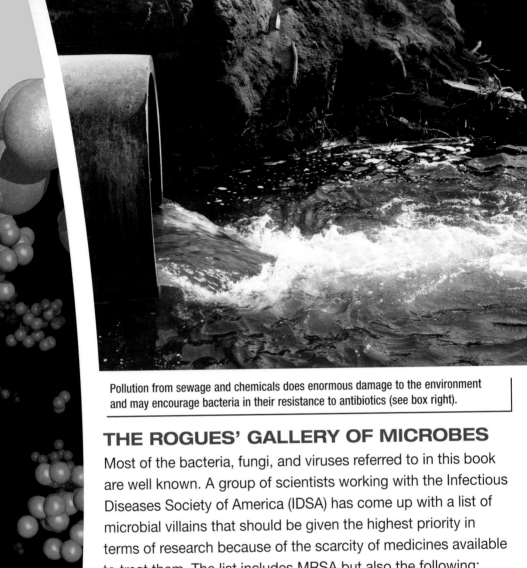

Pollution from sewage and chemicals does enormous damage to the environment and may encourage bacteria in their resistance to antibiotics (see box right).

THE ROGUES' GALLERY OF MICROBES

Most of the bacteria, fungi, and viruses referred to in this book are well known. A group of scientists working with the Infectious Diseases Society of America (IDSA) has come up with a list of microbial villains that should be given the highest priority in terms of research because of the scarcity of medicines available to treat them. The list includes MRSA but also the following:

- *Acinetobacter baumannii*: the fungus behind hospital-acquired pneumonia cases and infections in wounded U.S. soldiers
- *Escherichia coli* (E. coli) and *Klebsiella*: cause infections in the urinary tract, gut, and wounds
- aspergillus: a fungal infection that plagues people with weak immune systems such as those with HIV, cancer, or organ transplants, killing 50–60 percent of those it infects
- vancomycin-resistant *Enterococcus faecium*: a bug responsible for infections of the bloodstream, heart, and brain, among others
- *Pseudomonas aeruginosa*: a life-threatening bacterium that

E. coli can get into your stomach and intestines via undercooked beef.

especially affects patients with the lung disease cystic fibrosis

Alongside these top six, other microbes have shown increasing resistance in recent years. These include the following:

- *Shigella dysenteriae (S. dysenteriae)*: a form of dysentery that is a deadly disease in the developing world, killing many children
- *Streptococcus pneumoniae (S. pneumoniae)*: causes pneumonia
- *Haemophilus influenzae*: can cause meningitis in children
- *Neisseria gonorrhoeae*: a bacterium that is responsible for the sexually transmitted disease gonorrhea

INVESTIGATING THE EVIDENCE: IS POLLUTION DRIVING RESISTANCE?

The investigation: Scientists are researching the possibility that pollution from sewage sludge, animal slurry, disinfectants, and fabric softeners is linked to the way in which bacteria are resisting the effects of antibiotics.

The scientists: Dr. William Gaze, Professor Elizabeth Wellington, and Dr. Lihong Zhang from the University of Warwick, U.K., working with Professor Peter Hawkey from the University of Birmingham, U.K.

Collecting the evidence: The team gathered samples from areas of land where pollution was present and compared them with nearby soil and against samples that had had no contact with pollutants. The samples were frozen to minus 80 degrees Celsius and studied in a laboratory using molecular DNA analysis.

The conclusion: The millions of tons of sewage sludge and animal slurry spread on land every year contain resistant bacteria. The team found that this process is causing bacteria-carrying genetic elements that help resistance genes get into the soil and water.

WHERE DO WE GO FROM HERE?

The view that humans could conquer or dominate the world of microbes is looking at best optimistic and at worst arrogant as we come to the end of the first decade of the 21st century. Despite huge advances in medical science, common infections still kill millions of people, especially in the developing world.

From the 1970s until the 1990s, drug companies targeted diseases such as cancer, diabetes, and heart disease instead of developing new drugs. But the realization of the danger from resistant microbes has been heightened by the threat of a biological terrorist attack. More money is now being targeted at finding new ways to beat bacteria.

NEW IDEAS

Genetic engineering is being explored as one way to make bacteria more susceptible to existing drugs, and there is new research into an older technique involving antibodies. Antibodies are the body's own defense against an invasion, and they are found in serum, a component of blood. Serum therapy was used before antibiotics were developed, but there were side effects and toxic reactions. However, with the modern-day understanding of genetics and immunity, scientists have been able to update this therapy with some success. A drug called Synagis, which uses serum therapy to target a virus that causes serious respiratory infections in young children, is now in use.

Scientists are exploring many new avenues in order to tackle the problem of drug resistance. Over time, we can expect to see new drugs and treatments on the market. But will what we have learned about nature's ability to fight back be taken seriously in the future? The world is waking up to the fact that humans are only part of a complex and unimaginably diverse range of life that is struggling to survive on this planet. We may have to rethink our belief in our own superiority if we are to continue to stay in control.

Human serum contains salts, glucose, and other proteins, including antibodies formed by the body's immune system to fight infections.

antibiotic a medicine or chemical that can destroy harmful bacteria in the body

ART antiretroviral herapy—a treatment for HIV/AIDS

chemotherapy a treatment of a disease that uses chemicals

commensal describes a relationship among two or more species in which one or both species benefit from the other without causing harm

DDT an insecticide once widely used to repel malarial mosquitoes

derivative a substance or compound obtained from another substance or compound

disease an illness of humans, animals, or plants caused by an infection

DNA deoxyribonucleic acid—the chemical that carries the genetic material of a cell

E. coli a bacterium that normally lives in the human colon; most strains are harmless, but some are very dangerous

ecology the relationship between organisms and their environment

evolution the way in which living things change and develop over periods of time

fungus any of various types of organisms that get their food from decaying material or living things

genome the complete set of genetic material of a human, animal, plant, or other living thing

HIV/AIDS the human immunodeficiency virus (HIV) infects the cells of the immune system, destroying or impairing their function. Acquired immunodeficiency syndrome (AIDS) describes the most advanced stages of HIV infection.

immunity being protected against the damaging effects of a disease

latent describes a present but symptomless infection by a pathogen

lymphatic system a part of the immune system that helps the body fight infections

malaria a disease caused by a parasite that is transmitted from one human to another by the bite of infected anopheles mosquitoes

MDR-TB multidrug-resistant TB, which is resistant to a variety of the drugs usually used to treat it

microbe a tiny form of life such as a bacterium, fungus, or protozoan parasite

microbiologist a person who

studies the microbes that cause infectious diseases

microscope an instrument that uses lenses to produce magnified images of objects that are too small to be seen by the naked eye

mold a species of microscopic multicellular fungi; those that grow as single cells are called yeasts

MRSA methicillin-resistant *Staphylococcus aureus*—a type of staphylococcus, or staph, bacteria that is resistant to many antibiotics

mutation a permanent change in genetic material

nutrient a substance that is taken in by an organism and that promotes growth

organism any living thing that can survive independently

pathogen a microbe that can cause disease

plasmid a small circular piece of DNA found in bacteria and yeasts that is able to replicate independently

protozoan a member of a group of one-celled animals, some of which cause human diseases such as malaria

replication the reproduction of something by making an exact copy

resistant having the ability to resist (fend off) a disease or a drug

respiratory system the organs (parts) that are involved in breathing

side effects an unwanted effect from taking a medicine

sputum mucus and other material produced by the lining of the respiratory tract—also called phlegm; a sputum culture is used to test for tuberculosis

therapeutic concerned with the treatment of disease

tuberculosis (TB) a highly infectious disease caused by the organism *Mycobacterium tuberculosis*

vaccine a biological preparation that improves the immunity to a particular disease

virus a microscopic infectious agent that replicates itself only within cells of living hosts and that cannot survive independently

WHO World Health Organization—a United Nations (UN) agency that coordinates international health activities and helps governments improve health services worldwide

yeast any of various small single-celled fungi

AB

Alliance for the Prudent Use of Antibiotics (APUA) 49
American Pharmacists Association (APA) 55
animals 11, 13, 29–32, 51
anthrax 18
antifungals 19
antiretroviral therapy (ART) 8, 42–43, 45, 55
antivirals 19
antibacterial products 34–35, 49, 57
antibiotics 4, 7–8, 13, 16–24, 26–28, 30–33, 35–36, 38–40, 48, 50, 59–60
Black Death 54
blood poisoning 32

C

carbapenems 40–41
Chain, Ernst 19–20
chemotherapy 29
combination therapy 43, 55
common colds 13
computer modeling 15
cystic fibrosis 59

D

DDT 23, 44
diarrhea 4
diseases 4, 7–8, 11, 14–15, 18, 22–23, 30–31, 33, 42, 44–46, 56–57, 59
DNA 25, 59
dysentery 59

E

ecology 56
environment 7, 14, 25, 30–35
evolution 14

F

Fleming, Alexander 18–19, 23
Florey, Howard 19–20
food poisoning 32–33
fungi 11, 16, 19, 35, 57–58
future trends 52–60

G

gene therapy 54
genetic engineering 56–57, 60
genomes 25
"Get Smart" campaign 48
Global Advisory on Antibiotic Resistance Data (GAARD) 46
gonorrhea 59

H

HIV/AIDS 4, 8, 36, 42–43, 45, 54–55, 58
hospital-acquired infections (HAIs) 38, 50
hospitals 8, 24, 28–29, 38–39, 50–51

I

immune system 8, 25, 38, 40, 42, 58
infections 4, 9, 13, 18–20, 23, 27, 29–31, 33, 38–42, 44, 46, 49–51, 54, 58–60
Infectious Diseases Society of America (IDSA) 58
International AIDS Vaccine Initiative (IAVI) 54

L

latent bacteria 15, 36
Laveran, Charles 44
Leeuwenhoek, Anton van 18
leprosy 22
lymphatic system 36

MN

malaria 4, 8–9, 11, 14, 19, 22, 25, 44–45, 56–57
measles 4
meningitis 46, 59
microbes 10–15, 18–20, 23–29, 31–33, 35, 40, 46, 52, 56–60
microbiologists 18
monotherapy 43
MRSA 8, 13, 19, 27–29, 35, 38–39, 41, 50, 58
mucus 52
multidrug resistance 7, 36, 52
mutations 6–7, 15, 25, 43–44
nutrients 12, 33

P

pandemics 54

parasites 8, 11, 19, 25, 44–45, 57
Pasteur, Louis 18
pathogens 6–7, 15, 26, 28–29, 32–33, 35, 49
penicillin 19–22, 24, 28
physiology 56
pneumonia 4, 13, 46, 58–59
prescriptions 16, 26, 49
protozoans 11, 44

R

replication 36, 43
resistance 7, 14, 16, 19, 21, 23–28, 30–35, 40, 43–46, 48–49, 52, 54–55, 57, 59–60
respiratory system 16, 60

S

satellite tracking 45
selective pressure 14
self-medication 23
serum therapy 60
sewage 59
side effects 45, 55, 57, 60
smallpox 7
soil bacteria 7, 18, 59
sputum cultures 52
Stewart, William H. 23
superbugs 8–9, 13, 28, 38, 40
surveillance 46
swine flu 34
synthetic antibiotics 22

TU

therapeutic strategies 31, 33
traditional medicines 19
travel 40–41, 46
tuberculosis (TB) 4, 8–9, 15, 21–22, 36, 52
U.S. Centers for Disease Control (CDC) 46, 48, 50

VWY

vaccines/vaccinations 4, 22, 29, 36, 51, 53–54, 56–57
viruses 11–13, 19, 25, 34–36, 42–43, 49, 55, 58, 60
World Economic Forum 52
World Health Organization (WHO) 22, 32, 36, 45–46, 52
yaws 22
yeasts 11